5-Minute Messages for Children

By Donald Hinchey

Loveland, Colorado

Dedication

To Jennifer and Susan
and all the children of our church,
and to Margaret
who encourages the child in me.

5-Minute Messages for Children
Copyright © 1992 Donald Hinchey

Credits
Edited by Jolene L. Roehlkepartain and Lois Keffer
Interior designed by Dori Walker
Cover designed and illustrated by Liz Howe

Library of Congress Cataloging-in-Publication Data
Hinchey, Donald, 1943-
    5-minute messages for children / by Donald Hinchey
      p.   cm.
    Includes indexes.
    Summary: Presents brief interactive Biblical lessons on a variety of subjects, including faith, money, and Christmas.
    ISBN 1-55945-030-4
    1. Children—Prayer-books and devotions—English. 2. Church work with children. [1. Prayer books and devotions. 2. Christian life.] I. Title. II. Title: Five-minute messages for children.
BV4571.2.H55 1991
268'.432—dc20   91-44437
                                           CIP
                                           AC

14 13 12   03 02 01 00 99

Printed in the United States of America.
Visit our Web site: www.grouppublishing.com

Contents

Part One: Messages for Christian Living

Part Two: Messages for Experiencing the Bible

Part Three: Messages for the Seasons

4

Introduction

Making Children's Messages Meaningful

The children's message is an important part of many worship services. It gets children involved and provides adults with simple, straightforward, biblical applications. Children's messages also find an important place in Sunday school openings, children's church, church dinners and other church family-gatherings.

But too many children's messages are actually object lessons that say, "This object is like this truth." The problem with most object lessons is the presenter does the talking and the children just listen. The unspoken rule is: Be quiet and sit still.

Children like to talk, and they're always wiggling—so a good children's message should let kids talk and wiggle! The 52 messages in this book let children do just that.

Kids (and many adults) have trouble relating to lofty theological terms such as "substitutionary atonement." By beginning with a concrete experience, these messages enable children to make a leap in understanding that results in life-changing learning.

Making messages active and meaningful requires some careful planning. You'll need to take time to gather a few props and perhaps recruit a helper.

Encouraging children to participate in the message means you can't always control what they do or say. Children will tell you exactly what they think of your message as it's happening. During one of my messages, a child blurted out, "You know, Pastor, that's real dumb." Children's candor is fun and refreshing, and gives you further opportunities for teaching.

Message Ingredients

The 52 children's messages in this book contain some familiar and not-so-familiar ingredients. There's a scripture and a theme for each one. But many of these messages also call for helpers, games, props or souvenirs.

- **Helpers**—A children's message can be a skit that requires helpers. You can use an older child, a teenager or an adult. Make sure you inform your helper in advance.
- **Games**—The games included in these children's messages are all active. It may feel odd to play Red Rover or Hide-and-Seek during a children's message. But these games get kids involved. And they help children remember the message.
- **Props**—Whenever you use props, show them to all the children. Lift them high so the congregation can see. Keep a prop box in your office or closet.
- **Souvenirs**—Giving each child an item after the children's message can remind them of the message. It's best not to give souvenirs after each children's message, however, since children may begin to anticipate what they're going to get and miss the point of the message.

You can find items that would reinforce the message at your local Christian bookstore. Stickers, crosses, pencils with a message, and other give-away trinkets can be woven into the theme of your children's message.

Tips for Giving Children's Messages

The best place for children's messages is in front of the church where the congregation can see what's going on. The front of the church usually has space for children to move around. If you're using these messages in other settings, plan to have children gather at a place in the room where they can be seen clearly by the rest of the group.

It's a good idea to sit with the children. If you're on their level, they see you as a friend as well as a teacher, and you can interact with them more freely.

When you sit with children your voice may not carry well to the rest of the congregation. Tilt a standing microphone down to pick up your voice or use a lapel microphone. It's important for adults to hear, too.

Make it a habit to read the text straight from the Bible as you're giving these messages. This will be a good visual reminder to kids about how important and relevant God's Word is.

Don't always assume the senior pastor should give the children's message. Ask parents, professional educators, lay leaders and others who love children to give the children's message from time to time. Someone might want to take on this responsibility each week.

The 52 messages in this book range from simple messages that require no props, no helpers and no preparation to more elaborate presentations. Choose messages that best fit your needs. Feel free to adapt and change. Make these messages *your* messages. They're *not* meant to be read!

God's Word is liberating. Let the children in your church respond both faithfully and playfully, remembering we must all become as children to enter the kingdom of God.

Let the children come!

Part One:
Messages for Christian Living

1. What Jesus Says

Theme: Obedience; love

Bible Text:
I give you a new command: Love each other. You must love each other as I have loved you (John 13:34).

Preparation: None

The Message:

When your parents and I were kids, we used to play a game called Mother May I? all the time. The game was simple. The person who is the mother tells you to do something. Then you have to ask, "Mother may I?" Then the mother says, "Yes you may," and you can do it.

Sound simple? But if you don't say, "Mother may I?" you're out of the game. I'll be the mother. Here we go!

Give a series of commands such as "jump up," "sit down," "scratch your chin" and "shake hands with three people." Give the commands slowly at first and then faster and faster. Remove children from the game when they don't ask, "Mother may I?"

That's a hard game, isn't it? We get going so fast we forget to ask, "Mother may I?"

When Jesus talked to his disciples, he gave a simple command. *Read the text.* Jesus said, "Love each other." Period. You don't have to jump up or sit down or scratch your chin or shake hands with people. All you do is love each other.

That sounds simple, doesn't it?

Well, it isn't. In fact, sometimes that commandment is hard because some people are hard to love. And because we're sinners, we aren't able to love the way Jesus loves.

But, when Jesus says "love," and you ask, "Jesus may I?" Jesus will give you the power of the Holy Spirit to love just as he loves. So this week, love others just as Jesus wants us to. And ask him to help you do it.

Now I say, "Go back to your seats."
Children will ask, "Mother may I?"
Yes you may! Go in Jesus' love!

2. The Invisible Ball

Theme: Holy Spirit

Bible Text:
But the Spirit gives love, joy, peace, patience, kindness, goodness, faithfulness, gentleness, self-control (Galatians 5:22-23a).

Preparation: You'll need a large paper bag.

The Message:

I want to show you my invisible ball. *Hold out your empty hands, slightly cupped.* Isn't it beautiful? *Let children respond.*

What? You don't believe I have an invisible ball! Well, how can I show you?

I know, I'll throw the ball into the air and catch it in this bag. *Hold the large paper bag in one hand.* Then you'll believe me.

Throw the "ball" into the air. Follow it with your eyes. As the ball lands in the bag, snap your fingers with the bag held between your thumb and fingers. It sounds like something is falling into the bag.

Did you hear it? It's a heavy, invisible ball. Let's do it again.

Do this two to three times, each time tossing the ball higher in the air, following it with your eyes until it falls into the bag. Bounce the ball off a wall. Give the ball to a child to throw at you. Children will quickly get into the game.

That's an amazing ball, isn't it? You can't see it, but you know it's there by what it does.

I think that's what the Holy Spirit is like. We can't see the Holy Spirit, yet we know what the Holy Spirit does. The Spirit causes faith to grow in us. Galatians 5:22-23 says, "But the Spirit gives love, joy, peace, patience, kindness, goodness, faithfulness, gentleness, self-control." Even though we can't see the Holy Spirit, we know the Holy Spirit works among us by what we see, hear and know in our hearts.

3. Tug of War

Theme: Problems

Bible Text:

So what should we say about this? If God is with us, then no one can defeat us (Romans 8:31).

Preparation: You'll need a 20- to 25-foot rope or clothesline.

The Message:

L *ay the rope in a long line on the floor. Read the text.*

If God is for us, who can be against us? Paul, who wrote the book of Romans, is talking about a war. It's like the game Tug of War.

Let's play the game with boys against girls. Who do you think will win? *Let children respond.*

Okay, let's get all the boys on this side and two girls on this side. *Choose several boys and two of the smallest girls to play.*

H'mm. Something's not right here. There are only two girls versus all of these boys. We need some help. *Look over the congregation and choose two of the biggest men to help the girls.* (Names of the two men), would you please come here and help the girls?

Have the two men join the girls on their side of the rope. The boys will probably complain that this is unfair. Why is this unfair? There are still only two girls! *The boys will tell you the men are bigger and stronger.* Oh, now I see! It's like what the verse in Romans says. No matter how many problems we have, if we have God on our side, we'll win. When you have people as strong as (name the two men), you stand a good chance of winning.

Sometimes we feel there's too much ganging up on us. But God is on our side. And if God is for us, who can be against us?

4. Trust Walk

Theme: Trust; faith

Bible Text:

It was by faith Abraham obeyed God's call to go to another place that God promised to give him. He left his own country, not knowing where he was to go (Hebrews 11:8).

Preparation: You'll need a blindfold for each child. (Cut up an old sheet to make blindfolds.) If there are a lot of children in the congregation, ask someone to help you during the message.

The Message:

Once there was an old man named Abraham and he had an old wife named Sarah. Now when people grow older they want to live where they've always lived and do some fun things. But God had another idea for Abraham and Sarah.

God told Abraham and Sarah it was moving time. He wanted them to pack up everything and move. Do you know where to? *Children will probably shake their heads.*

Well, they didn't either. God didn't tell Abraham and Sarah where to move. God just said to move. *Begin passing out a blindfold to each child.* There was no road map, no travel schedule. Just pack up and move. *Read the text.*

Now that requires trust. What is trust? *Let children respond.*

Trust is when you love someone so much, and you know that person loves you so much, that you'll do just about anything that person asks you to do. Right now I'm going to ask you to put on these blindfolds and follow me. Do you trust me?

Have older children help the younger children put on the blindfolds. Line up children across the front of the congregation. If you have a large number of children, make two lines and ask the helper to lead the second line.

No peeking now. Let's each put our hands on the shoulders of the person in front of us. Here we go!

Lead children down one aisle of the church and up another. If you have two lines, have the helper take his or her line on a different route through the sanctuary. If there's sufficient space between pews, lead children down an empty aisle. As you walk, tell more about the story of Abraham. Occasionally ask children how they're doing.

So Abraham left his home and land and went with God to a faraway country. I'll bet there were days when Abraham wondered where God was leading him. Is that what you're wondering? *Let children respond as you lead them to the front of the church.*

Abraham followed God, and soon God led Abraham to Canaan. God told Abraham that Canaan was his new home.

Well, here we are home again. Take off your blindfolds. I'm happy you trusted me enough to take that walk with me. How did it feel? *Let children respond.*

In a way, life is a trust walk. Sometimes we don't know where we're going, but God is in front of us, leading and caring for us. God will always be with us, and we can trust him no matter where we go and what we do.

I'd like you to keep your blindfold with you this week as a reminder that although we don't know where we're going, God is going with us. And we can walk in faith.

5. The Making of a Saint

Theme: Saints

Bible Text:
Paul and Timothy, servants of Christ Jesus, to all the saints in Christ Jesus at Philippi (Philippians 1:1a, NIV).

Preparation: You'll need a white robe, a halo made out of Christmas garland, a large Bible, a large cross and a box to put everything in.

The Message:

Today let's talk about saints. Some churches in our town are named after saints. What is a saint? How do you make a saint? *Let children respond.*

I need someone who would like to be made a saint. Who feels "saintly" today? *Choose a child. Place him or her on a high place, such as on a sturdy chair, where everyone can see.*

Now let's take out my saint kit. *Take out the box and show it to the children.* Let's see what we can do. *Take out the robe.* Everyone knows saints wear robes. We see that in the pictures of saints all the time. *Put the robe on the child.* Now, do you feel like a saint? *Let the child respond.*

We still need something more. How about a halo? Everyone knows saints need halos.

Put a halo on the child's head. Step back and look at the child. H'mm. I don't think (say the child's name) is quite a saint yet.

Oh I know—a Bible! Saintly people read the Bible. So, here's a Bible. *Give the child a Bible to hold.*

What do you think? *Let children respond.* Now, do you feel real saintly? *Let the costumed child respond.*

I don't know. You still look like (say the child's name) to me except that you're dressed funny. I don't think we did a great job of making you a saint. *Have the costumed child sit down next to you.*

Maybe that's because we can't make saints. Only God can. *Read the text.*

God makes saints by using one thing we don't have here. *Take out the cross from the box.* And that's the cross. God makes us saints by the cross. When Jesus died on the cross, he took away our sins and made us new people before God.

That's really what saints are—God's special friends. We can become saints if we accept what Jesus did for us by dying on the cross and then rising from the dead. Anyone can be a saint when they follow Jesus' teaching.

We may not always act like saints. I'll bet not even Saint (say the name of the costumed child) acts like a saint all of the time. But God still loves us. We saints are not perfect people, but we are forgiven and loved by God.

6. Travel Light

Theme: Materialism

Bible Text:

Don't carry any money with you—gold or silver or copper. Don't carry a bag. Take for your trip only the clothes and sandals you are wearing (Matthew 10:9-10a).

Preparation: You'll need a backpack, sleeping bag, clothes, some junk food, a radio, a portable television and books.

The Message:

When *children are settled, read the text.* Who likes to hike in the woods? *Let children respond.* I just love to go backpacking in the woods, and today I'd like to give you a quick backpacking lesson. But first, I need someone to help me. Who will help me? *Choose a small child.*

The first thing you do before you go backpacking is to choose what you need to take with you. What do we really need?

A backpack is a good place to start. *Put the backpack on the child.* Sleeping bag? That's good. *Give the child the sleeping bag to hold.* What else? Clothes. *Stuff clothes into the backpack and wrap clothes around the child.*

Now what? Food? Yes, we can get really hungry. *Take out the food you brought. Talk about each food item as you stuff it into the child's backpack.*

What next? Oh, I know. We'd better not lose touch with the world. We need a radio in the woods, don't we? *Put a radio into the backpack.*

But television is nice, too. We can't miss our Saturday-morning cartoons. *Bring out the portable television and set it in front of the child.*

What about books? I've got some good ones here. *Put several books in the child's arms. Then stand back and look at the overloaded child.*

Something's wrong here. What is it? *Let children respond.*

Of course! That's the problem. When you have so much, you have a hard time moving! That's why Jesus told his disciples to travel light—not to take more than you need.

Think of what you really need to be happy. My guess is that it's very little. And God will take care of us without all the junk we pile on ourselves.

7. The Healing Touch

Theme: The power of touch

Bible Text:
A ruler from the synagogue, named Jairus, came to that place. Jairus saw Jesus and bowed before him. The ruler begged Jesus, saying again and again, "My little daughter is dying. Please come and put your hands on her. Then she will be healed and will live" (Mark 5:22-23).

Preparation: None

The Message:

Think about how many different kinds of touch there are. There's touch that's not so nice, such as hitting, pinching or poking. Why do people hit and pinch and poke? *Let children respond.*

Then there's playful touch like tickling. *Tickle a child.* There's mussing up hair. *Muss up another child's hair.*

Then there's loving touch. Sometimes when someone is sad and you don't know what to say, you might just put your hand on that person's arm. *Put your hand on a child's arm.* That helps the person feel better.

But if you really love someone, what would you do? *Let children respond.* That's right—a hug! *Give a child a big hug.*

We don't need words to let people know how we feel about them. Touches are ways of talking without words. *Read the text.* The dad in this story knew if Jesus touched his little girl, she would get better. And you know what? This dad was right! When Jesus touched the girl, she got well and sat up. Jesus healed with his touch.

We may not be able to heal with our touch, but we *can* make people feel better by giving them a hug or a pat on the back. When we use touch like Jesus did, people will know how much we care for them.

When you get back to your seat, give your mom or dad or sister or brother a big hug. Let them know with your touch you love them.

8. The First Will Be Last

Theme: Being number one

Bible Text:
So those who have the last place now will have the first place in the future. And those who have the first place now will have the last place in the future (Matthew 20:16).

Preparation: Choose two adult helpers prior to the worship service.

The Message:

Who wants to be first? *Choose three of the biggest children.* That's great. You're the first. Doesn't it feel great to be first? Now who wants to be second? *Choose two children.* Now who wants to be last? *Choose a small child to be last.*

Talk to the "firsts": Since you wanted to be first, get down on your hands and knees. *Have your helpers line up the children shoulder to shoulder, facing the congregation.* Okay, those who were the "seconds" get to climb up on the firsts. Spread your knees so you balance on the firsts.

Make sure the pyramid is sturdy before putting the last child in place. And now for the last. *Lift the last child to the top of the pyramid.*

Ask the firsts on the bottom: How are you doing? How does it feel to be first? *Have the helpers work with you to disassemble the pyramid.*

I guess we all want to be first. But Jesus tells us the first will be last and the last will be first. *Read the text.* That's like the children who wanted to be first ending up on the bottom of the pyramid. Jesus wants us to be first in that way—supporting others and holding them up when they have problems. You firsts did just what you were supposed to do! We're proud of you!

Although Jesus is Lord, he became last for us. He died on the cross for us. So when we're tempted to want to become boss over everyone, think about it. Those who are first hold up everybody else!

9. A Place for Everyone

Theme: Self-esteem

Bible Text:

All of you together are the body of Christ. Each one of you is a part of that body (1 Corinthians 12:27).

Preparation: Ask the choir director to have the choir prepare a simple, familiar, four-part song for the message.

The Message:

Have the children gather in front of the choir. Each of us has different but special talents. And while your talent (name a child sitting near you) is not the same as your talent (name another child), that talent is just as important. As a matter of fact, when we use our talents together, we can make beautiful music.

That's the way a choir is. A choir is made up of four different parts. There's the bass section. These men sing really low. Let's hear the bass section. *Basses sing a low note.*

Then there are the tenors. They sing a little higher than the basses. *Tenors sing a note above the basses.*

The women with low voices are called altos. *Altos sing a note.*

And finally, way up on top, are the sopranos. *Sopranos sing a note.*

Now what if the basses decide that only they should sing? Here's how it would sound. *Basses sing the chosen song with only their part.*

Or what if the tenors say the basses sing too low and only the tenors should sing? *Tenors sing the song with only their part.*

What if the altos insist on singing alone? *Altos sing only their part of the song.*

Since the sopranos usually sing the melody, they might think they're the most important and they should sing by themselves. *Sopranos only sing.*

That's what some people do, you know. We forget God gave us all different talents. We sometimes think only our talent is the one that counts. Or we may think someone else's talent is better than our talent.

No matter how big or small you are, God made you very special. And God wants you to use the gifts he gave you.

I think it's time for the choir members to use all their talents at the same time. Let's stand and direct the choir as they sing together.

The choir sings the song.

Isn't that wonderful? Every choir member used his or her voice to praise God. That's what we can do, too. *Read the text.* No matter who you are or how different you are, God has a place for you. All you have to do is use the talent God gave you.

10. Shoelaces

Theme: Serving

Bible Text:

John answered everyone, "I baptize you with water, but there is one coming later who can do more than I can. I am not good enough to untie his sandals. He will baptize you with the Holy Spirit and with fire" (Luke 3:16).

Preparation: Before the children's message begins, untie your shoelaces. Ask one child who's coming up for the talk to untie his or her shoelaces.

The Message:

Before you start the message, find the child who has untied shoelaces. *Do not point out the child to the other children.*

Once there was a man named John. Now John was a big, strong man. He wore animal skins and ate bugs.

But John was also a humble man. He was a servant. When he told people about Jesus, he said, "I am not good enough to untie his shoelaces."

In Bible days, servants helped people tie and untie their shoes. But John said he wasn't good enough to untie Jesus' shoes.

I think we could say that, too. We're not good enough to be Jesus' servants. Jesus is so great, and we're not. But Jesus suffered and died for us, so we should always want to serve him.

Jesus told us one way we could serve him is by serving others. I think shoelaces are a good reminder of that. I notice a lot of children walking around with their shoelaces untied. They could trip and fall. But sometimes they like their shoelaces untied because it's cool.

To remind us that we're Jesus' servants, tie up somebody's shoelaces. *Go to the child with the untied laces and tie them.*

If that person asks what you're doing, explain you're a servant. And while you may not be good enough to tie up Jesus' laces, you are good enough to be a servant.

So keep your eyes open this week for untied shoelaces. Remember John, and remember Jesus. Tie up those shoelaces!

11. Money Talks

Theme: Money

Bible Text:
Your heart will be where your treasure is (Matthew 6:21).

Preparation: You'll need a crisp one dollar bill.

The Message:

Have you ever heard people say, "Money talks"? It means if you have money to spend, people will listen and do what you want. There's another way money talks. The way we spend our money tells people a lot about us!

If this dollar bill could talk, what would it say about you? If you spent this dollar on candy, what would it say about you? *Let children respond.*

If you dug a hole and buried this dollar, what would that tell people? If you ripped the dollar into tiny pieces and threw it around, what would people think? *Let children respond.*

If you bought treats with this dollar and invited all of your friends over, what would it say about you? If you gave the dollar to a homeless person to buy food, what would that say about you? Or if you dropped this dollar bill into our offering plate this morning, what would it say about you? *Let children respond.*

Read the text. Jesus meant that the way we spend our money tells what we think is important. Jesus never tells us exactly how we should spend our money. But he expects our love for him to help us decide how to spend our money. Jesus is the most important person in the world, and we want to please him when we spend our money.

Our money isn't really *our* money. It's a gift from God. God gives us money so we can live and have fun and help other people. So listen to your money. Listen to what it tells you about yourself.

12. How Do You Get Up to Heaven?

Theme: Heaven

Bible Text:
For God loved the world so much that he gave his only Son. God gave his Son so that whoever believes in him may not be lost, but have eternal life (John 3:16).

Preparation: You'll need a step ladder, a can of food, a red construction paper heart, an offering plate and a Bible.

The Message:

Where's heaven? *Let children respond.*
Nobody really knows exactly where heaven is. Some people think heaven is way up in the sky. Others think heaven is in outer space. I don't know where heaven is. It's pretty confusing.

Most people think of heaven as "up there." Some people think if you do good things, you can climb a ladder by yourself and make it to heaven. These people think if you do good things, such as feeding the poor *(have a child put the can of food on the bottom ladder step)*, that will get you closer.

If you love someone *(have a child put the red construction paper heart on the next step)*, you might move a little closer. If you go to church and give money *(have a child place the offering plate on the next ladder step)*, then you'll move up another notch. And if you read the Bible every day *(have a child put the Bible on the next step)*, you'll get even closer.

See how it goes? People believe if you do good things and love God, you might be able to climb up that ladder and live with God forever.

There are some real problems with that.

27

The ladder leading up to heaven has a lot of steps. We could never do enough to make it to the top. And we may do good things *only* to get to heaven. God doesn't like that. God wants us to help people because we really care about people.

So God had a better idea. Jesus came down the ladder and became a baby at Bethlehem. Because we couldn't climb up the ladder to heaven, God came down.

Now we can give our food to the poor because we love them. *Take the food off the ladder.* We can love other people because God loved us first. *Take the heart off the ladder and give it to a child.* We can give our money to the church because God gives us so much. *Take the offering plate off the ladder and put some money into it.* And we can read our Bibles to learn more about God. *Take the Bible off the ladder and open it.*

We can't climb the ladder to heaven.

Instead, God came down the ladder. John 3:16 says: "For God loved the world so much that he gave his only Son. God gave his Son so that whoever believes in him may not be lost, but have eternal life."

13. Jesus Joggers

Theme: Christian living

Bible Text:

Brothers, I know that I have not yet reached that goal. But there is one thing I always do: I forget the things that are past. I try as hard as I can to reach the goal that is before me. I keep trying to reach the goal and get the prize. That prize is mine because God called me through Christ to the life above (Philippians 3:13-14).

Preparation: None

The Message:

*A*s you read the scripture aloud, have children do stretches and deep knee-bends. Now let's do a little jogging—a little Jesus jogging. That's the kind of jogging Paul talks about in the Bible verses I just read.

Let's jog in place because our church really isn't that big. *Jog in place.*

It's a great day for a jog, isn't it? Paul once said that when he ran, he always ran with his eyes open. What do you think would happen if we closed our eyes while we ran? Let's try it. *Jog in place with your eyes closed.*

Oops! We can bump into each other if we don't keep our eyes open.

Paul also says we must never look back when we jog for Jesus. What do you think would happen if we all looked over our shoulders while we ran? Let's try it. *Jog in place while looking over your shoulder.*

Nope. We've got to keep looking ahead—otherwise we could fall.

Paul warns about running crooked. Some people get off course when they run. But Paul says we need to try to reach the goal. What would happen if we ran crooked? Let's try it. *Jog in place crookedly.*

We'd better keep running straight ahead. Hey! I see the finish line! Let's run faster. *Jog in place faster.* We made it! We won! We won!

Whew! I'm out of breath. Let's sit down. Actually, we didn't win the race. Jesus won it for us by dying on the cross. Now we can run our part of the race by living the way Jesus wants us to. Then we can win the prize of living forever in heaven with Jesus.

Remember the three things Paul tells us about running the race of life: Run with your eyes open. Never look back. And always run straight ahead toward Jesus.

14. Hide-and-Seek

Theme: Shame

Bible Text:

Then they heard the Lord God walking in the garden. This was during the cool part of the day. And the man and his wife hid from the Lord God among the trees in the garden. But the Lord God called to the man. The Lord said, "Where are you?" (Genesis 3:8-9).

Preparation: None

The Message:

How many of you like playing the game Hide-and-Seek? Let's play it right now. Not "It"! *If some children don't know how to play Not "It," explain the last person to say "Not 'It' " is "It." And "It" gets to hide.*
Okay, let's all shut our eyes for 10 seconds while (name of the child who is "It") hides. You can't leave this room, (name of the child who is "It"). If we can't find (name of the child) in one minute, (name of the child) wins! *Shut your eyes. Count aloud slowly to 10 while the child hides.*

Now let's look. *Look for the child who hid. If you can't find the child within a minute, call out the child's name and resume the message.*

That was fun. Hide-and-Seek is one of the oldest games we have. In fact, the game goes back to the Garden of Eden! Adam and Eve played Hide-and-Seek with God! Listen. *Read the text.*

Isn't that silly? How can you hide from God? God knows where we are all of the time, but Adam and Eve were so ashamed of disobeying God they hid from him.

We do that, too. When we do naughty things, we hide from God. We act just like Adam and Eve. We think God will be angry with us and punish us.

But God came looking for Adam and Eve. God wasn't going to be left out of their lives because he loved them too much. And God loves us, too.

Hide-and-Seek is a fun game, but it's not fun to hide from God. Besides, God will come searching for us to love and forgive us.

15. The Awesome Mosquito Bite

Theme: Suffering

Bible Text:
We have sufferings now. But the sufferings we have now are nothing compared to the great glory that will be given to us (Romans 8:18).

Preparation: Put a pair of winter gloves, a large bandage and a piece of candy in a box.

The Message:

Who has ever had a mosquito bite? What's it like to have a mosquito bite? *Let children respond.*

You scratch and scratch, but that only makes it itch more. Then your dad or mom says, "Don't scratch your mosquito bite." You try not to scratch, but the more you think about it, the more it itches. Your little mosquito bite becomes an awesome mosquito bite.

What can you do? Let's pretend (name a child near you) has a mosquito bite on the arm. What can we do? *Take the gloves from the box and give them to the child.*

You can wear gloves. That way you can't scratch the mosquito bite. Except now your hands get sweaty. And the mosquito bite still itches.

Maybe a bandage would help. *Put a bandage on the child's arm.* Does that solve it? Probably not. You know what's under that bandage, and you still want to scratch it!

Do you know what works? Candy. *Take out the candy.* You take a piece of candy and you think of how good it will taste. Then you pop it in your mouth and you taste that yummy candy. Then you forget about your mosquito bite. And when you forget it, it doesn't itch anymore!

In Romans 8, Paul says: "We have sufferings now. But the sufferings we have now are nothing compared to the great glory that will be given to us."

Paul was talking about a bigger problem than a mosquito bite. But the way to solve the problem is still the same. When we think about something good—such as how much Jesus loves us—then our problems don't seem so big.

When we have a problem, whether it's a mosquito bite or a cold or a family member who's in the hospital, Paul wants us to remember that God is Lord over everything. And that includes mosquito bites and messy problems. Think about everything God has done for you, and your problems may not seem so awesome.

16. A 120-Pound Wallet

Theme: Giving

Bible Text:
I taught you to remember the words of Jesus. He said, "It is more blessed to give than to receive" (Acts 20:35b).

Preparation: You'll need your wallet, a sock to put pennies in, as many pennies as you can gather and a suitcase.

The Message:

Do any of you have wallets? Let's see them. *Look at the wallets children show you.* I have a wallet. I carry it every day. I put money in it. *Show your money.* I carry papers in it. *Show your papers.* And there are pictures of my family. *Show children the pictures.*

I like my wallet because it fits in my pocket (or purse). It's nice and light, and it doesn't weigh me down. What if I became rich? I'd have to carry my money in something bigger. *Take out the sock full of pennies.* This weighs a lot! *Let children feel the weight.* I think this could still fit into my pocket (or purse). *Squeeze the sock into your pocket or purse.*

If I got even richer, I'd need a bigger wallet. *Take out the suitcase.* I'll bet this new "wallet" could weigh 120 pounds! How would I carry this around? *Let children respond.*

There's nothing wrong with being rich. But being part of the kingdom of God means putting God first. One problem for the rich is putting money before God. It's hard to help others when you have to carry around a 120-pound wallet! But what if I had all this money? What could I do so it wouldn't weigh me down? *Let children respond.* That's right.

Read the text. I can share it with others. That's why I'm giving you each a penny to put in your pocket this week. *Pass out pennies.* When you feel this penny, remember you don't need a lot. And when you get more pennies, think about giving.

17. Special People

Theme: Self-esteem

Bible Text:
So you should know that the true children of Abraham are those who
have faith (Galatians 3:7).

Preparation: You'll need a sticker for each child.

The Message:

This is a time to honor special people. Let's see. People who are
having birthdays are special. Is there anyone here who is having a
birthday this week? How about this month? You are special! Let's
give you a sticker and a round of applause. *Lead the applause.*

My special calendar also says this is the day to honor short-haired
children. Are there any short-haired children here? You get a special
sticker and a round of applause. *Lead the applause.*

Did you know this is national blue-shirt week? Anyone wearing a
blue shirt is special. You get a sticker and a round of applause. *Lead the
applause.*

Well, that's it. I guess some of you are special and some of you aren't
so special, right? *Let children respond.*

Paul used to have that problem in his church. Some people said they
were special because they were children of Abraham. They thought God
loved them more than other people. But Paul said, "So you should know
that the true children of Abraham are those who have faith." That means
all people who love and trust God are special.

God has given each of you special gifts. *Name a couple of children
sitting near you and the things they do well.* But what makes all of us
special is that Jesus loves us. That means each one of you is very, very
special.

That's why each one of you should have a sticker. *Give a sticker to each child who hasn't received one.* And I think we should give all of you a round of applause for being so special. *Lead the congregation in applause as children go back to their seats.*

18. Moving Day

Theme: Sadness

Bible Text:
Jesus said, "Don't let your hearts be troubled. Trust in God. And trust in me" (John 14:1).

Preparation: You'll need a couple of moving boxes, a few toys and a marker.

The Message:

How many of you have ever moved? *Get responses.* How did you feel when you moved? *Let children respond.*

There's a lot of work involved in moving. First, you have to get boxes. *Pick up the boxes to show the children.* Then you take all of the stuff out of your room and put it into the boxes. *Put toys into the boxes.*

Then you have to mark the boxes. *With a marker write "stuff" on the boxes.* And soon a huge truck pulls up in front of the house. Some huge men walk in and begin moving your boxes out. And you wonder if you'll ever see your toys again.

When the truck is loaded, you look around your old room. And it's empty. It's sad. But the saddest part is when your friends say goodbye to you. What other times have you felt sad? *Let children respond.*

Jesus also felt sad. Jesus knew he would be leaving his friends when he said in John 14:1: "Don't let your hearts be troubled. Trust in God. And trust in me."

When you feel sad, what do you do? *Let children respond.* The best thing to do is to tell Jesus about your sadness. Then tell others how you feel. There's nothing wrong with feeling sad.

So the next time you move, say goodbye to someone or just feel sad, tell God about it. Talk to a friend or someone in your family. Then remember Jesus says to trust in him when you feel sad.

19. Clean Up Your Room!

Theme: Obedience

Bible Text:
If you love me, you will do the things I command (John 14:15).

Preparation: Make a large sign that says, "THOU SHALT CLEAN YOUR ROOM." Make smaller signs that say, "For Your Health," "Shame," "Fear," "Greed" and "Love."

The Message:

Do your parents ever say this to you? *Hold up the large sign that says, "THOU SHALT CLEAN YOUR ROOM." Ask older children to read it aloud.*

In some homes, this is the 11th commandment. If you leave a mess in your room, the parent says, "Thou shalt clean your room."

Now you may wonder why you should clean your room. You could say this. *Hold up the sign and have children read with you: "For Your Health."* When rooms get dirty, there are lots of nasty germs crawling around. So you clean your room for your health.

Or you could clean your room for this reason. Read with me. *Hold up the "Shame" sign.* You'd be ashamed if visitors dropped in and looked into your messy room. What if Uncle Frank and Aunt Helen saw your room and said, "You should be so ashamed"?

Here's another reason to clean your room. Let's read together. *Hold up the "Fear" sign.* If you don't clean your room, your parents will punish you. Now that's scary.

Or you could clean up your room for this reason. *Hold up the "Greed" sign and have children read it aloud.* Now that's a good reason. If you clean your room, your mom will give you a double banana split.

But the best reason to clean up your room is this. *Hold up the "Love" sign.* That's right—love. You know you make parents happy when you clean your room. And you make parents even happier when you clean your room before you're asked.

In John 14:15, Jesus says, "If you love me, you will do the things I command." Likewise, if we love our parents, we'll do things they want us to do.

We can show our love by doing things before we're asked. We can pick up our rooms. And we don't need to clean our rooms for these reasons. *Show the signs: "For Your Health," "Shame," "Fear" and "Greed."*

But if we clean our rooms and do other things out of love *(hold up the "Love" sign)*, we'll keep Jesus' commandments.

20. Shout Those Praises!

Theme: Praise

Bible Text:
All you nations, praise the Lord. All you people, praise him. The Lord loves us very much. His truth is everlasting. Praise the Lord! (Psalm 117).

Preparation: None

The Message:

In the Old Testament, there's a short chapter. It's Psalm 117, and it has only two verses.

Although Psalm 117 is a short chapter, the message is important. It says: "All you nations, praise the Lord. All you people, praise him. The Lord loves us very much. His truth is everlasting. Praise the Lord!"

Now how can we praise the Lord? *Let children respond.* Yes, we can sing. We can shout. We can praise God in a lot of different ways. Let's try some. Let's stand and praise God by whispering loudly. Let's all whisper, "Praise God." *Whisper loudly.*

We can shout praises, too. Let's all shout: "Alleluia! Praise God!" *Shout.*

Does anyone know a song that praises God? *Have children tell you songs. Choose one and sing it together.*

We can praise God by giving God a standing ovation. Let's all clap and get everyone in the congregation to give God a standing ovation. *Start the clapping and signal people to stand.*

And we can jump up and down and shout: "Praise God! Praise God!" at the same time. *Jump and shout praises.*

We can get really creative in the way we praise God. But the important thing is to remember to praise God. So let's shout one more praise before we go back to our seats. *Shout, "Praise God!"*

21. Junk Food

Theme: Jesus

Bible Text:

Then Jesus said, "I am the bread that gives life. He who comes to me will never be hungry. He who believes in me will never be thirsty" (John 6:35).

Preparation: You'll need a picnic basket. Fill it with a paper plate, a doughnut, a soft drink, potato chips, candy and a brownie.

The Message:

What if you came to dinner one night and your mom or dad said: "Guess what's for dinner tonight? Your favorite!" After you guessed and guessed what was for dinner, your mom or dad took out a doughnut. *Take out the doughnut and put it on the plate.*

What do you think would be best to drink with a doughnut? *Let children respond.* How about some soda pop! After you ate this meal, how do you think you'd feel? *Let children respond.*

What if the next night you saw that potato chips were being served for dinner! *Put the potato chips on the plate.*

The third night you'd get candy! Now what would you think? *Put the candy on the plate and let children respond.*

Maybe by the fourth night you'd ask, "Could I please have some vegetables and some chicken?" But instead you got a brownie. *Put the brownie on the plate.*

It's crazy to think your parents would give you a meal like this, isn't it? What would happen if we ate only junk food? *Let children respond.*

Both God and your parents know we eat good food to keep healthy. That's why we eat vegetables, fruits, meats and breads.

Do you know what else will keep us healthy? Jesus. Jesus calls himself the bread of life. *Read the text.*

That doesn't mean we eat Jesus. No. That's not what Jesus means when he says he's the bread of life. Jesus says he's the bread of life because people who believe in him and follow him will live forever.

We don't need junk food. We need Jesus who is the bread of life. And when we stick with Jesus, we'll be healthy Christians.

22. Time Out

Theme: Rest

Bible Text:
By the seventh day God finished the work he had been doing. So on the seventh day he rested from all his work (Genesis 2:2).

Preparation: None

The Message:

Let's all stand and run in place as fast as we can. Ready? Go. *Run really fast for 15 seconds. Then have the children stop.*
Who's tired? I'm kind of tired. And I know I would be really tired if we kept running like that for 10 minutes or more. So let's sit and rest. *Sit.*

Do you ever get tired? When? *Let children answer.* I get tired sometimes, especially when I have a lot of work to do.

Sometimes, I even get tired after I play all day. Has anyone felt that way? *Let children respond.*

What do you do when you're tired? *Let children respond.* The best thing to do when you're tired is to rest. And sometimes you need to rest even if you don't feel tired.

When God made the Earth, he worked hard. For six days, God made rivers, animals, people and plants. God was busy. But what did God do on the seventh day? *Read the text.*

God rested. God took it easy. And we should, too.

So make time to rest and to worship God each week. Then you can keep going strong the rest of the time.

23. Red Rover

Theme: Fighting

Bible Text:
Holy Father, keep them safe by the power of your name (the name you gave me), so that they will be one, the same as you and I are one (John 17:11b).

Preparation: None

The Message:

C lear an 8- to 10-foot space in front of the sanctuary. Jesus once prayed to his father that his followers would all be one. That meant Jesus wanted his followers to stick together and not fight. Let's listen to Jesus. *Read the text.*

I know one thing that keeps people from being together—it's something like the game Red Rover. Who knows how to play Red Rover? *Let children respond.*

Let's show the congregation how to play Red Rover. I need eight children. Who would like to play? *Choose four children to play on each team. Have the children form two lines facing each other. Have the children in each line hold hands.*

Now we need one line to call a child from the other line like this: "Red Rover, Red Rover, send (name a child) right over." And (name of the child) will run as fast as he or she can to try to break through the line. Okay? *Motion to one team.* Call someone over.

If the person you call breaks through the line, that person gets to choose someone to take back to his or her line. But if the person you call doesn't break through the line, he or she has to join that team. *Let children play Red Rover for two or three turns.*

The goal of Red Rover is to break up teams. And that can be a fun game. Let's stop the game and sit down.

It's not so fun when breakups happen in real life. When families fight and get broken up, it makes Jesus sad. When friends get mad and fight, Jesus is sad. Jesus wants us to stick together. He doesn't want us to fight and then break up.

Just like in Red Rover, we've got to stick together so we can stay together. We've got to hold tightly to one another and to Jesus. Then we won't break apart.

Part Two:
Messages for Experiencing the Bible

24. Going the Other Way

Theme: Running away

Bible Text:

The Lord spoke his word to Jonah son of Amittai: "Get up, go to the great city of Nineveh and preach against it. I see the evil things they do." But Jonah got up to run away from the Lord. He went to the city of Joppa. There he found a ship that was going to the city of Tarshish. Jonah paid for the trip and went aboard. He wanted to go to Tarshish to run away from the Lord (Jonah 1:1-3).

Preparation: None

The Message:

Read the text. *What's going on here? Let children respond.* The Bible says Jonah wanted to run away.

Let's understand what happened here. Let's pretend Nineveh is that way. *Point in one direction, and have the children run to that side of the church.* Now that's where God wanted Jonah to go. But do you know where Jonah went? He went that way. *Point in the opposite direction, and have children run to that side of the church. Then call them back to the center.*

Jonah didn't want to do what God wanted, so he ran away. What do you think of that? *Let children respond.*

It's not good to run away, but sometimes we feel like doing it. Have you ever thought about running away? When? *Let children respond.*

What do you think happened to Jonah when he ran away? *Let children respond.* Yes, he got swallowed by a big fish.

What should Jonah have done instead? *Let children respond.* Jonah should have talked to God about the way he felt. He should have told God: "I don't think this is a good idea. Why do I have to do this? Why is this so important?" Then God could have explained why it was important for Jonah to go to Nineveh.

It's important to obey our parents and teachers, too. Have you ever been asked to do something and you didn't do it? What happened? *Let children respond.* The worst thing would be to run away. That's not good.

So let's not do what Jonah did. Let's do what we are told. And when we're not sure why we're supposed to do something, let's ask. Okay?

25. Night Lights

Theme: Fear

Bible Text:

The Lord is my light and the one who saves me. I fear no one. The Lord protects my life. I am afraid of no one (Psalm 27:1).

Preparation: You'll need a flashlight.

The Message:

Who's afraid of the dark? Raise your hand if you are. *If not all the children raise their hands, say:* I'll bet that all of you are afraid of the dark. At least sometimes.

There are times when I'm afraid of the dark. Most adults get scared of the dark at times. When it's really dark outside without the moon or stars or any kind of light, lots of people—even big people—get scared.

Let's all lie on the floor. Then close your eyes and pretend it's really dark.

Now let's imagine it's late at night and we're getting ready to go to sleep. You've been kissed good night. You've said your prayers. You're just lying there in the dark.

Then you hear a creak outside your window. What could it be? *Let children respond.*

Then you yell, "Bring me a night light!"

Turn on the flashlight. Open your eyes!

Whew! This night light saved the day—I mean night. Who has a night light in their bedroom? *Let children respond.*

Night lights are great. When it's dark, this little light helps us see there really are no (mention the fears children named earlier). The night light helps us see there's nothing to be afraid of. The night light helps us sleep.

The Bible tells us God is a night light. *Read the text.* Sometimes the light is bright, like when the shepherds were in the fields outside of Bethlehem watching their flocks.

Other times God's light is soft. It's like a night light. It gives us just enough light to see we don't have to be afraid.

God promises to be with us at all times. God is with us during the day and in the night. So we don't need to be afraid of the dark. Because if God is our night light, what do we have to fear?

26. Irresistible Words

Theme: God's Word

Bible Text:
When your words came, I ate them; they were my joy and my heart's delight (Jeremiah 15:16a, NIV).

Preparation: You'll need a box of Alpha-Bits cereal and a paper plate.

The Message:

*P*our some Alpha-Bits cereal onto a paper plate as children walk forward for the children's message.

What's great about this Alpha-Bits cereal is you can eat it *and* learn from it. You can spell words in your bowl and then eat them. It drives your folks crazy, but it's kind of fun to do. I'm going to spell some words. *Spell simple words such as "cat" and "big." Then eat the words.*

Yum. That tastes good. Let's see what other words you can make. *Let several of the older children make words and then eat them.* How does that taste? How does it feel to eat Alpha-Bits cereal? *Let children respond.*

Jeremiah 15:16 says, "When your words came, I ate them; they were my joy and my heart's delight."

Do you think people had Alpha-Bits when the book of Jeremiah was written? *Let children respond.* I don't think so.

Eating the words we make with Alpha-Bits can make us happy. But reading God's Word can make us happy, too. Who likes to listen to stories read aloud? *Let children respond.* Why do you like to hear stories read aloud? Why do you like to read? *Let children respond.*

God's Word is just as fun to read as the other books we read. God's Word is full of wonderful stories. God's Word tells us God loves us and forgives us and wants to be with us forever. God's Word says some neat things!

But what if we never open the Bible? *Let children respond.* If we never read God's Word, we won't know what God says. We'll miss out on a lot. God's words won't make us happy if we don't take time to read them.

We need to take the cereal off the shelves and get some food inside of us every morning! And we need to take the Bible off the shelf so we can read God's Word.

So get reading. And you'll get happy about God's Word.

27. A Tour of God's House

Theme: Church

Bible Text:
I was happy when they said to me, "Let's go to the Temple of the Lord" (Psalm 122:1).

Preparation: None

The Message:

How many of you have ever taken a tour? *Let children respond.* Where have you taken a tour? *Let children respond.* You can take tours of museums, homes and different places you go on vacation. It's fun to take a tour because you can find out a lot of things you didn't know before.

Today, we're going to take a tour of our church building. Do you know why we want to do this? Let's read what the psalmist says. *Read the text.*

Let's start at the door. *Lead the children to the main door where most people enter your sanctuary.* When we come into church, we're entering an exciting place. The door is an important part of the church because if you don't walk through it, you'll never learn how important God's house is.

Lead children to the main musical instrument in your church. Another important part of the church is music. Psalm 149:1 says: "Praise the Lord! Sing a new song to the Lord. Sing his praise in the meeting of his people." Music helps us praise God. And this (name the instrument you're pointing at) helps us praise God.

Lead children to the altar. In Old Testament times, the altar was a place of sacrifice. "Sacrifice" means to give something up. In Old Testament times, the pastor would put an animal on the altar as a sacrifice to show God how much the people loved him. That's why we bring our money offering to the altar. We're sacrificing something we own to give to God. The altar is also a place where we sometimes come to offer prayers to God.

Lead children to the pulpit. This is the place where the pastor preaches the sermon. Each Sunday, the pastor tells us about something from God's Word. This pulpit reminds us we come to church to hear good news.

Lead children to the place where the congregation sits. This is where people sit to hear God's Word and to praise God. This is an important part of the church, because if we didn't give people a place to sit, they wouldn't come.

Lead children to other areas of your church building that are important to your tradition. Explain what those areas are and why they are important.

Lead children to the front of the church. We've finished our tour of the church. Thanks for taking the tour with me.

When we started our tour, we heard a Bible verse. I'll say it and then I would like you to say it with me. *Reread the text. Then repeat it two or three times with the children.*

We're glad when we come to God's house. We're glad that you are here!

28. God's Tattoo

Theme: Love; self-worth

Bible Text:

But Jerusalem said, "The Lord has left me. The Lord has forgotten me." The Lord answers, "Can a woman forget the baby she nurses? Can she feel no kindness for the child she gave birth to? Even if she could forget her children, I will not forget you. See, I have written your name on my hand" (Isaiah 49:14-16a).

Preparation: None

The Message:

Do your parents tell you not to write on your hands with a pen? *Let children respond.* That's good advice.

Do you know why that's good advice? Other than the fact your hand would get dirty, you could get an infection if you get a cut. It's not a good idea to write on yourself with a pen.

Then there are tattoos. Do you know what a tattoo is? *Let children respond.* Yes, a tattoo is a picture that some people have drawn on their skin.

Some people get flowers put on their skin. Some people have the names of their girlfriends or boyfriends drawn on their skin.

The thing about a tattoo is once it's on your skin, it's hard to get off. In fact, it's almost impossible to get off. So if you get a tattoo, you'd better be ready to wear that tattoo for life.

Isaiah talks about God having a tattoo. Can you imagine that? How could God have a tattoo? *Read the text.*

See! We are God's tattoos! God loves us so much that he has our names written on his hand. And God sees our names every day. God will never forget us, no matter what.

We may not feel important sometimes. But God thinks we're

important enough to keep each of our names tattooed on his hand—forever!

Let's look at the palms of our hands now. If we look closely at all the lines in our palms, we can see the tattoo God gave us. How many of you see a cross? *Let children respond. If some children have difficulty seeing a cross, you might want to show them the cross in your palm or in the palm of a child whose cross is easy to see.*

That's our tattoo. That cross on the palms of our hands reminds us that Jesus died on the cross for us. And that cross can help us remember God has our names written on his hand, and he will never forget us.

29. How Do You Close a Banana?

Theme: Forgiveness

Bible Text:
I will forgive them for the wicked things they did. I will not remember their sins anymore (Jeremiah 31:34b).

Preparation: You'll need a banana, paper clips, glue and tape.

The Message:

Don't you just love bananas? A banana is one of God's great treats. A banana looks beautiful. *Hold up the banana for everyone to see.*

You can make yummy foods with bananas. You can make banana cookies, banana bread and banana cream pies. And bananas are good for you.

What's more, God made bananas so you can take them with you wherever you go. You can eat bananas on a picnic. Or you can eat bananas as a snack when you're out for a walk. See how easily a banana can be opened. Would someone like to help me peel this banana? *Invite a child to peel the banana slowly. Take a bite from the banana and show how good it is.*

But there's a problem with bananas. If you eat only half a banana and want to save the rest, it's hard to close it. Bananas don't come with Velcro or zippers! Let's see if we can close this banana.

Show children the paper clips, glue and tape that you brought. Invite children to use these items to close the banana.

How about these paper clips? Will that work? Let's try a little glue. Maybe that will help. Or how about if we tape the banana back together?

Nope. There's nothing you can do to close a banana! Once it's opened you just have to eat it.

There are things in life like that, too. Sometimes we say something mean to someone we love. We may say, "I hate you!" And once we say something like that, we wish we could take what we said, put it back in our mouth and seal it up. But like the banana, it's too late. We can't seal our mouth back up.

So what can you do if you hit someone or you say something mean?

The book of Jeremiah tells us. *Read the text.* God knows we can't take back the sin we've done, so he forgives us. God sent his son into the world to die for our sins. So when we do something wrong, we can ask God to forgive us.

I think trying to close a banana is silly. It's just about as silly as trying to fix our sins ourselves. Instead we need to ask God to forgive us. Because once we're forgiven, we can get back to enjoying the great world God made—including bananas!

30. The Wheat-and-Weeds Rap

Theme: Faith sharing

Bible Text:

Then Jesus told them another story. He said, "The kingdom of heaven is like a man who planted good seed in his field. That night, when everyone was asleep, his enemy came and planted weeds among the wheat. Then the enemy went away. Later, the wheat grew and heads of grain grew on the wheat plants. But at the same time the weeds also grew. Then the man's servants came to him and said, 'You planted good seed in your field. Where did the weeds come from?' The man answered, 'An enemy planted weeds.' The servants asked, 'Do you want us to pull up the weeds?' The man answered, 'No, because when you pull up the weeds, you might also pull up the wheat. Let the weeds and the wheat grow together until the harvest time. At harvest time I will tell the workers this: First gather the weeds and tie them together to be burned. Then gather the wheat and bring it to my barn' " (Matthew 13:24-30).

Preparation: Rehearse the rap.

The Message:

Read the text. This story is a parable. And sometimes parables are hard to understand. So I'm going to tell this story as a rap. And I need your help.

At the end of each verse, I need you to say: "Grow seed! Grow seed! Grow seed! Grow!" The first time you say, "Grow seed!" stretch your arms and hands to the right. The second time you say, "Grow seed!" stretch your arms to the left. The third time you say, "Grow seed!" stretch your arms to the right. Then when you say "Grow!" throw your arms and hands straight above your heads. Okay? Let's try it. *Go through the motions and words a few times to teach the children. Then begin the rap:*

A farmer went out to his field to sow,
To scatter the seed and watch it grow.
But in the night, his enemy,
Came sneaking in,
With a bushel of weeds!
The children say this part: Grow seed! Grow seed! Grow seed! Grow!
He watched and waited for a week or two,
And up from the soil came the tiny shoots.
But oh my! He couldn't believe,
Mixed with the wheat,
Were those ugly weeds!
The children say this part: Grow seed! Grow seed! Grow seed! Grow!
His servants came by, a scratchin' their heads,
"You've got weeds in the field," one said.
"That enemy's tryin' to ruin the crop."
The other servants said,
"We'll pull them up!"
The children say this part: Grow seed! Grow seed! Grow seed! Grow!
"Oh no," said the master. "We must retreat!
When you pull up the weeds, you'll ruin the wheat!
We'll let them grow 'til harvest day,
And then we'll haul,
Those weeds away."
The children say this part: Grow seed! Grow seed! Grow seed! Grow!
Now the moral of this gospel rap,
Is Satan sets an awful trap.
He'd have us judge who's good or bad,
Divide the church,
That makes God sad!
Instead, our Lord says, "Leave it to me.
I'll judge you all for eternity.
The wicked will burn when this age is done,
But you righteous will shine,
Like the morning sun." So.
The children say this part: Grow seed! Grow seed! Grow seed! Grow!
End of rap.
We can't decide who will make it to heaven and who won't. Our job is
to tell everyone about Jesus and how much he loves us. Then we can
say: "Grow seed! Grow seed! Grow seed! Grow!"

31. Come to the Party!

Theme: Celebration

Bible Text:

The kingdom of heaven is like a king who prepared a wedding feast for his son. The king invited some people to the feast. When the feast was ready, the king sent his servants to tell the people to come. But they refused to come to the feast. After that, the king said to his servants, "The wedding feast is ready. I invited those people, but they were not worthy to come. So go to the street corners and invite everyone you see. Tell them to come to my feast" (Matthew 22:2-3, 8-9).

Preparation: Before the worship service, arrange for three adults to make up an excuse when you call on them. You'll need party decorations and tape.

The Message:

Do you like to go to parties? Today we're going to have a party. *Have the children help you put up a few decorations.* Now, who could we invite to the party? *One by one, call on the adults you talked to before the service. Act disappointed when they refuse.*

This is terrible! I have this party ready, but nobody wants to come. What should I do? I know what I'll do. I'll invite you to the party! Would you like to come? *Let the children respond.* That makes me very happy. You know Jesus told a story about a king who invited his friends to a party. But no one could come. *Read the text.*

Jesus invites us all into God's kingdom like the king invited people to his party. And God wants everyone to come. But a lot of people say no. They make excuses. So they don't come.

When we say yes to God's invitation, God is happy. He likes it when people want to come to his kingdom. So don't make excuses. Say yes to God's invitation.

32. Hats

Theme: Jesus' suffering and death

Bible Text:

Then they used thorny branches to make a crown, and they put it on his head. Then they called out to him, "Hail, King of the Jews!" (Mark 15:17b-18).

Preparation: You'll need as many different kinds of hats as you can find. Find some hats that represent a profession, such as police hat or firefighter hat. Then make a crown of thorns from a thorn bush.

The Message:

Today let's talk about hats. People wear hats for different reasons. Do you like to wear hats? *Let children respond.*

Some people wear hats just to keep their heads warm. *Take out a winter cap and put it on a child's head.* Others wear hats because they look pretty. *Pull out a pretty hat and put it on your head.*

Others wear hats because everyone else wears hats. *Pull out a common hat, such as a baseball cap. Put it on a child's head.*

Some hats let you know what people do. *Pull out hats from certain professions. Describe them and then put the hats on children's heads.*

Describe any other hats you may have. Put them on children's heads.

I have one hat left. Who do you think would wear a hat like this? *Take out the crown of thorns and hold it up for everyone to see.*

This is a strange hat. Does it protect you? No. It hurts. Does it tell what kind of work you do? *Let children respond.*

I guess in a strange way it does. This is like the hat Jesus wore on the cross. *Read the text.* The people who made it for him said it was a crown. But it's not a crown I would want to wear if I were king.

Let's remember this week how much Jesus loved us. He loved us so much he wore this crown of thorns. Jesus suffered and died—just for us.

33. Storms

Theme: Fear

Bible Text:

They went in the boat that Jesus was already sitting in. There were also other boats with them. A very strong wind came up on the lake. The waves began coming over the sides and into the boat. It was almost full of water. Jesus was at the back of the boat, sleeping with his head on a pillow. The followers went to him and woke him. They said, "Teacher, do you care about us? We will drown!" Jesus stood up and commanded the wind and the waves to stop. He said, "Quiet! Be still!" Then the winds stopped, and the lake became calm. Jesus said to his followers, "Why are you afraid? Do you still have no faith?" (Mark 4:36b-40).

Preparation: Memorize the songs used in this message. Ask a man to be Jesus for this message.

The Message:

We're going on a boat trip with Jesus and the disciples today. How many of you have ever been in a boat? *Let children respond.* Let's all face this wall and pretend we're in a boat. Let's invite (name the man) to pretend to be Jesus and sit in the back of the boat.

Jesus once took his friends on a boat trip. When they started, it was a pretty day. The disciples were happy, so they sang a song.

Sing this song to the tune of "Row, Row, Row Your Boat." Row, row, row your boat, gently on the seas. With Jesus in the back of the boat, life is such a breeze.

Suddenly a wind came up. And the waves became choppy. *Rock up and down. Encourage the children to do the same. At this time your adult "Jesus" should be sleeping in the back of the boat.*

But the disciples still sang their song. Row, row, row your boat, gently on the seas. With Jesus in the back of the boat, life is such a breeze.

Then the wind grew stronger. *Rock harder side to side. Encourage the children to do the same.* And stronger. *Rock more.* Soon everyone was so scared they couldn't sing their pretty song. Instead they sang this song.

Sing this song to the tune of "Row, Row, Row Your Boat." Save, save, save my boat, I'm drowning on the seas. I'm so scared! I think I'll die! Jesus, help me please!

The disciples then turned to look for Jesus. *Point to your Jesus sleeping in the back of the boat.* But Jesus was asleep! The disciples were so afraid, but Jesus wasn't scared. He was asleep.

Let's wake up Jesus. *Have the children shake Jesus and yell at him to wake up. Slowly he wakes up.*

When Jesus woke up, he wasn't happy with his disciples. But he stood up and told the storm to stop. The wind then stopped and everything became calm. The disciples were amazed.

The real Jesus is Lord over all the storms of life. When we're upset and feel like we're going up and down and up and down, Jesus will smooth things out. When we're scared, Jesus will take away our fears.

I can see the shoreline now. Let's sing our song. *Encourage the children to sing with you.* Row, row, row your boat, gently on the seas. With Jesus in the back of the boat, life is such a breeze.

34. Called by Name

Theme: Names

Bible Text:
The man who guards the door opens it for him. And the sheep listen to the voice of the shepherd. He calls his own sheep, using their names, and he leads them out (John 10:3).

Preparation: You'll need a book of baby names.

The Message:

Do you know that one of the most important things about you is your name? I would guess your family thought hard about what to name you because a name is important.

I have a book that tells the meaning of names. It tells me what my name means. *Give the meaning of your first name.* Who would like to know what their name means? *Give the meanings of three or four children's names.*

There's another reason why names are important. When people know your name, they care about you. They've taken time to remember your name. They just don't call you, "Hey, you!"

The Bible says Jesus knows your name! *Read the text.* Jesus knows (mention specific children's names) and loves these children just as they are. In fact, Jesus loves you so much he died on the cross for you. And when we die, we'll go to heaven and we'll be welcomed by name!

35. Foot Washing

Theme: Servanthood

Bible Text:
Then he poured water into a bowl and began to wash the followers' feet. He dried them with the towel that was wrapped around him (John 13:5).

Preparation: You'll need a bucket, warm water and some towels.

The Message:

Earlier in the service, announce that all children who want to come to the children's message are invited to remove one shoe and one sock. Do you know what these are? *Show the bucket, water and towels, and let children respond.*

Jesus used these things. *Read the text.* When Jesus was on Earth, people didn't wear shoes. They wore sandals. After walking around on dusty roads, their feet would be very dirty.

So servants would wash the feet of the family and their guests. Do you think you'd like the job of foot-washer? *Let children respond.*

I don't think I would. But Jesus did. And Jesus washed his disciples' feet to show that he was a servant. *Lead children to the bucket. Have them hold on to your shoulders as you wash their feet. As you do this, tell more about Jesus washing the disciples' feet.*

Most people don't want to be servants. They want to be the boss! But Jesus tells us to be servants. He wants us to help each other and serve people.

What do you think it would be like if you kept a bucket of water by the door of your house and washed everyone's feet as they came in? *Let children respond.* It probably wouldn't work well. But we can do other things to serve others. What could we do? *Let children respond.*

Those are good ideas. Let's serve each other just like Jesus served his disciples. And when we help others, Jesus will be happy.

36. The Jesus Club

Theme: Discipleship

Bible Text:
All people will know that you are my followers if you love each other (John 13:35).

Preparation: You'll need some uniform parts from children's organizations, such as Girl Scouts or baseball teams.

The Message:

How many of you belong to a club? *Let children respond.* A club is a group of people who think the same way and do the same things. People in clubs are good friends. They often wear the same things. You know people in clubs by what they wear.

For example, if you were wearing this, what club would you be in? *Hold up one of the uniform items. Let children respond. Repeat this exercise using clothing or props from children's organizations in your community.*

Now what would children wear to identify themselves as Christians—as part of the Jesus Club? *Let children respond.*

Christians don't have to wear uniforms, do they? We Christians don't wear special hats. But people can still know we're a part of the Jesus Club. Let's read John 13:35 to see what we need to do to be part of the Jesus Club. *Read the text.*

So how do people know that you're a part of the Jesus Club? Because you love each other! You can show love by caring for people when they're sad. You can be a friend to someone who's lonely. You can help the poor and the homeless. And when you do these things, people will say, "I bet that child is a member of the Jesus Club!"

So how will people know we're Christians? If we love one another just as Jesus loved us.

37. Christian Pizza

Theme: Church

Bible Text:
You believers are like a building that God owns. That building was built on the foundation of the apostles and prophets. Christ Jesus himself is the most important stone in that building (Ephesians 2:20).

Preparation: You'll need a table, a premade pizza crust, canned pizza sauce and pizza toppings.

The Message:

L et's think about the church today. Listen to this verse from Ephesians. *Read the text.*
     The building this verse talks about refers to all Christians. There are different nationalities, races and languages. But one thing is the same. We all believe Jesus is our savior.

I think the church is like a pizza! *Point to your pizza ingredients.* The church needs a good strong crust. *Hold up the crust.* Ephesians tells us Jesus and the apostles are the foundation of the church. The foundation is the bottom part, the thing that holds all the ingredients together. The foundation of a pizza is the crust.

Now for the sauce. Who'll help me pour the sauce? *Invite two children to pour the sauce onto the crust.* The sauce is what gives the pizza taste. And sauce is full of good things that make us healthy. Sauce is like the Bible. It's full of things that are good for us.

You can put a lot of other things on pizza. *Ask two more children to help.* All these toppings are different. Each has a distinct taste. But together, all these toppings make a yummy pizza.

There are lots of different kinds of Christians, and God loves us all because we have the same foundation—Jesus.

Now let's add the cheese. That will hold all the toppings together, just like the Holy Spirit holds us together in the church.

Well, I think the pizza is done. Let's remember that although Christians can be different, everyone has something to offer. Together, we make up one church, just like all our ingredients make up one pizza.

38. Training Wheels

Theme: God's presence

Bible Text:
God is strong and can help you not to fall (Jude 24a).

Preparation: You'll need a child's two-wheel bicycle with a pair of training wheels attached.

The Message:

How many of you can ride a bike? *Let children respond.* Are you really good at riding a bike? Have you always been good at riding a bike? *Let children respond.*

What was it like the first time you rode a bike? *Let children respond.* What if you had these? *Point to the training wheels.* How did you feel when you had training wheels? *Let children respond.*

Training wheels are wonderful things. They balance the bicycle so you won't fall off. Who wants to try out the training wheels? *Help a small child onto the bicycle. Let the child ride the bicycle.*

With training wheels you know you won't fall. And when you don't fall, you feel more sure of yourself. And soon you can ride on just two wheels.

God's help is like training wheels. *Read the text.* When we think something bad will happen, God will be there to help us. When we get older, we still need God. God always acts like a pair of training wheels. He's there to hold us up when we think we're going to fall.

39. The Spirit Who Won't Blow Away

Theme: Holy Spirit

Bible Text:
I will ask the Father, and he will give you another Helper. He will give you this Helper to be with you forever (John 14:16).

Preparation: You'll need a cupcake, matches and four non-extinguishable candles.

The Message:

Did you know the church has a birthday? The New Testament talks about the time when the Christian church was born and the Holy Spirit came. I have a cupcake here to celebrate the birthday of the church and the coming of the Holy Spirit. Let's light the four candles. *Invite an older child to help you light the candles.*

Now let's sing the birthday song. *Sing "Happy Birthday to You" to the church with the children.* Let's blow out the candles. *Try blowing out the candles. They'll continue to relight. Ask children to try. Be careful since some children can become ambitious in blowing out the candles.*

We can't seem to get the fire out.

That's how it is with God's Spirit, too—God's Holy Spirit. You can't put out the light. The devil keeps trying, but he can't do it either. The Holy Spirit's light keeps burning and burning.

Read the text. Jesus promises he will send us the Holy Spirit, which he calls a helper. This Holy Spirit is with us every day.

Point to the cupcake. These are trick candles, of course. They're made to burn again and again. But there's nothing tricky about the Holy Spirit. The Spirit will burn brightly within us if we let him. And no one can blow him out!

Part Three:
Messages for
the Seasons

40. Ways to Say "I Love You"

Theme: Valentine's Day; love

Bible Text:

Dear friends, we should love each other, because love comes from God. The person who loves has become God's child and knows God. Whoever does not love does not know God, because God is love (1 John 4:7-8).

Preparation: None

The Message:

What gifts do people give on Valentine's Day? *Let children respond.* When people love each other, they like to give each other gifts. But there's a problem with this. Sometimes people think you have to give presents to show love.

But we can show love in different ways. We can say, "I love you" with words. Try this with me. *Say, "I love you" a number of times with the children.* That's easy, isn't it?

We can show people we love them by listening to them. You've been listening to me talk for a few minutes now, and I'm glad you've given me that gift. When we listen to people, we say, "I love you."

Or how about this? *Choose a child you know well and give that child a hug.* Hugs are great ways to tell people you love them. And you don't even have to use words.

Helping people is another way to say, "I love you." How can we help people? *Let children respond.*

Why is it important to love each other? Let's see what the Bible says. *Read the text.* What was the one big way Jesus showed his love for us? By dying on the cross. He gave the best gift of love. He gave himself.

Think of ways you show love to others. You can give hugs. You can say loving words. You can help people. There are so many ways to say, "I love you." And the best gifts aren't always the ones that cost the most.

41. Dandelions

Theme: Spring; thankfulness

Bible Text:
Let's come to him with thanksgiving. Let's sing songs to him (Psalm 95:2).

Preparation: You'll need a dandelion for each child.

The Message:

*A*s children come up for the children's message, give them each a dandelion. I was in a field, and I picked some flowers for each of you. Aren't they pretty? *Let children respond.*

Of course, they're just dandelions. And some people think dandelions are weeds. They pull them up from their lawns and throw them away.

Dandelions are everywhere. And since we get used to them, we forget how pretty they are. Dandelions remind us winter is over and spring is here.

God gives us so many good things. But since these good things are around us all the time, we sometimes forget about them. And we sometimes forget to thank God for things like this.

Our families are always there, so we may forget to thank God for our families. Our schools and teachers are always there, so we may forget to thank God for them. We also sometimes forget to thank God for the food on the table, the clothes we wear and the home we live in. We expect these things to be there—just like the dandelions—and we forget to thank God for them.

There's a Bible verse I'd like to teach you. *Read the text. Repeat it several times with the children.*

This spring, I want you to notice the dandelions. They remind us that spring is here, and they remind us to thank God for giving us so many good things. It's good to give thanks to God!

42. April Fool

Theme: Easter; April Fools' Day; tricks

Bible Text:

The angel said to the women, "Don't be afraid. I know that you are looking for Jesus, the one who was killed on the cross. But he is not here. He has risen from death as he said he would. Come and see the place where his body was" (Matthew 28:5-6).

Preparation: You'll need two tricks from a novelty store.

The Message:

Do you know what next (name the day of the week April 1 falls on) is? *Let children respond.* It's April 1. Do you know what happens on April 1? *Use one of your tricks on the children.*
April fools!

Or, what if it's April 1 and someone does this to you? *Describe what someone may do. Use another one of your tricks.*
April fools!

These are called practical jokes because they're not meant to hurt anybody. And people laugh when a trick is played on them. On April 1, it's fun to play harmless jokes on people. These jokes remind us we need to laugh at ourselves.

At this time of year, we remember when God played a trick on the devil. Listen. *Read the text.* The devil thought he had won when Jesus died on the cross. The devil must have laughed when the disciples were crying about Jesus' death. But when the angel rolled the stone away, the devil wasn't laughing.

Jesus' resurrection was no joke! God raised Jesus from the dead, and we never have to fear death. And we never have to be afraid of the devil again, either. What a great trick on the devil! Christ is risen! He is risen, indeed!

43. The Pretzel's Message

Theme: Good Friday; the Crucifixion

Bible Text:
But Christ died for us while we were still sinners. In this way God shows his great love for us (Romans 5:8).

Preparation: You'll need a large box of twisty pretzels.

The Message:

*A*s children come for the children's message, give them each a pretzel and tell them not to eat it yet.
I've given you each something you've seen before—a pretzel. *Hold up one of the pretzels.* A long time ago in Germany, Christian families wouldn't eat eggs or drink milk during the season of Lent, which is right before Good Friday. Instead of eating bread, people ate pretzels.

Look closely at your pretzel. *Point out the cross in the middle.* There's a cross in the middle of the pretzel. If you put the pretzel on your lap and cross your arms over your chest, you'll make the same cross over yourself that you see on the pretzel. *Demonstrate by placing your right hand on your left shoulder and your left hand on your right shoulder. Do this with the children.*

Good Friday is the day we remember the cross. Jesus came into our world to die for us. He took our sins with him to the cross. *Read the text.*

We remember the cross in all kinds of ways on Good Friday. Eating some pretzels would be a good reminder of what Jesus did on the cross.

You can use some string and wear a pretzel as a necklace. If your classmates at school ask you why you're wearing a pretzel, you can tell them about the story of the pretzel. And you can tell them about what happened on Good Friday.

So think about the pretzel's message. Think about Jesus dying on the cross—just for you!

44. Who Will Roll Away the Stone?

Theme: Easter; the Resurrection

Bible Text:
Very early on that day, the first day of the week, the women were on their way to the tomb. It was soon after sunrise. They said to each other, "There is a large stone covering the entrance of the tomb. Who will move the stone for us?" (Mark 16:2-3).

Preparation: Before the service, have a very heavy stone (that requires at least two adults to carry) placed in front of the altar.

The Message:

I nvite children to sit around the stone. Who put this stone in front of our altar? Did you, (name a child)? *Ask a few other children.*

I know this is Easter, but why is this stone here? Maybe the Bible can tell us. *Read the text.*

The Bible tells us about an Easter stone. And I think this is an Easter stone. But we can't just leave it here. It doesn't look nice. Let's move it. *Ask a small, young child to move the stone. The child should not be able to move it.*

Let's get more help. *Choose another small child to help the other child. If the stone is heavy enough, two children won't be able to move it.*

This is a big problem. Who will roll away the stone? That's the question Mary Magdalene and her friends asked as they walked to the tomb on that Easter morning. The stone that sealed Jesus' grave was very heavy. They knew they couldn't move it. And they wondered how they would get in to take care of Jesus' body.

But then you know what happened? The Bible tells us there was an earthquake! The whole earth shook and an angel rolled the stone away. Then the angel sat on the stone. The angel told the women Jesus had risen from the dead.

Let's leave this stone in front of the altar for the rest of the service. It will remind us that Jesus is alive!

45. Seeing Is Believing

Theme: Easter; believing

Bible Text:
Then Jesus told him, "You believe because you see me. Those who believe without seeing me will be truly happy" (John 20:29).

Preparation: You'll need a live kitten or chick to put in a box with breathing holes poked through. Or, you can put a goldfish in a plastic bag with water before putting it in a box. Whatever animal you choose, make sure it can breathe and the children can't see it.

The Message:

It's Easter! It's time to remember Jesus rose from the dead for us. And because Jesus rose from the dead, we can have eternal life. We can't prove we have eternal life because we can't see it. But we can believe it because that's what Jesus told us.

It's like when someone makes you a promise. For example, I promise you I have a live animal in this box. It's beautiful. Do you believe me? *Let children respond. Most will say they believe you.* Why? *Let children respond.*

You believe me because you trust me. Even though you don't see what's in the box, you believe.

That's what we do with Jesus, too. Even though we didn't see Jesus rise from the dead, we believe he did. We don't have to see it to believe it.

Thanks for listening to my children's message this morning. You can return to your seats. *Most children will be reluctant.*

What's wrong? I said you could go back to your seats. *Children will say they want to see what's in the box.*

But I thought you said you trusted me. You believed me. *Children will say they still want to see what's in the box.* Do you mean you don't believe me? *Children will point out they believe you, but they just want to see.*

I understand. That's the problem Thomas was having when the disciples told him they'd seen Jesus. Thomas wanted to see Jesus for himself.

I bet you still want to see what's in the box, right? *Take out the animal and show the children.*

Now we can believe because we've seen. But Jesus says it's good to believe when you don't see. And that's what we do with Jesus! So keep on believing.

46. I'm Thirsty!

Theme: Summer; people's needs

Bible Text:

A brother or sister in Christ might need clothes or might need food. And you say to him, "God be with you! I hope you stay warm and get plenty to eat." You say this, but you do not give that person the things he needs. Unless you help him, your words are worth nothing (James 2:15-16).

Preparation: You'll need a pitcher of Kool-Aid, an empty glass and a stack of paper cups. Before the service, ask three older children to beg for a drink during the children's message. Practice the whole message with them if possible. Do this message on a hot summer day.

The Message:

It sure is hot today, isn't it? It's almost too hot to talk. But let's read what the Bible has to say. *Read the text. As you read, pour a glass of Kool-Aid. Take a long drink. Then fill the glass again. The children who have been cued to beg, should begin to whine, "I'm thirsty!"*

Shh! Let's listen to the Bible verse. It's very important. It's about people who need something, but we don't give it to them. *Take another drink of Kool-Aid. The children should whine louder.*

When we say we have faith *(take another sip)* and yet don't help people, it's like we don't mean what we say we believe. *Take another drink. Children should beg for something to drink.*

I do wish you would behave yourselves. You're ruining a good Bible lesson! It says here if someone says they're hungry *("or thirsty," the children say)*, you should give them something to eat *("or to drink," the children say)*.

Now I get it! You're telling me I should listen to you instead of just telling you about this Bible verse.

It's easy to forget the needs of people around us. The Bible wants us

82

to remember we need to put our faith into action. We need to do what we believe.

This week pay attention to what people around you need. When you help them, you're doing what Jesus did! Now what did you say you needed? *Children should say, "Something to drink!"*

We've got some cups of Kool-Aid here. Let's all have a cold drink while the congregation sings our next hymn.

47. Name That Saint

Theme: St. Nicholas' Day; gifts

Bible Text:
Thanks be to God for his gift that is too wonderful to explain
(2 Corinthians 9:15).

Preparation: You'll need candy, nuts and small toys in a bag to put in children's shoes during the message.

The Message:

As Christmas comes to our country, children get excited about Santa Claus. It's fun to think of a nice old man who brings us presents.

But on December 6 in Europe, children believe another old man comes to help them celebrate Christmas. Let's play a guessing game. When you know who this man is, raise your hand. Don't tell any one his name! Just raise your hand. Let's play Name That Saint!

Here's the first clue. This man was a bishop, which meant he was like a pastor. He wore a long robe and carried a staff. He had a long white beard. He wore a tall, beautiful hat. Can you name that saint? *Let children raise their hands if they know. Remind them not to tell the name.*

Here's clue number two. Legend says one time when this man was at sea, a bad storm came. The sailors thought they were going to drown. But this saint was so brave he saved all the sailors in the boat. Can you name that saint? *Let children raise their hands if they know. Remind them not to tell the name.*

Here's the third clue. This man was very giving. There are stories about how he gave a lot of money to a young lady so she wouldn't have to marry a man for money. Can you name that saint? *Let children raise their hands if they know. Remind them not to tell the name.*

Okay, one more clue. Children in Europe believe on December 6 this saint comes to your house. If you leave a shoe outside your door, he will fill it with goodies. Can you name that saint? *Some children may know. Encourage them to shout the name.*

Yes! It's St. Nicholas.

The real St. Nicholas lived a good life serving God's people. He was kind and giving. And he always told people how much Jesus loved them. *Read the text.*

Sometimes we can forget that at Christmas time. Christmas is Jesus' birthday. Christmas is a good time to love people, to give gifts and to tell people Jesus was born on Christmas. That's what St. Nicholas did. And that's why we should think about him at this time of year.

If you'll each take off a shoe right now, I'll pretend I'm St. Nicholas and fill it with good things. *Drop candy, nuts and small toys from your bag into children's shoes as they hold them up to you.*

48. Getting Ready for Christmas

Theme: Advent; preparing

Bible Text:
About that time John the Baptist came and began preaching in the desert area of Judea. John said, "Change your hearts and lives because the kingdom of heaven is coming soon." John the Baptist is the one Isaiah the prophet was talking about. Isaiah said: "This is a voice of a man who calls out in the desert: 'Prepare the way for the Lord. Make the road straight for him' " (Matthew 3:1-3).

Preparation: Have a well-known adult in your church do this message with you. Make a photocopy of this message and have that person memorize the "helper" parts of the dialogue. You'll need a vacuum cleaner.

The Message:

It's Advent. Only (name the number of days) more days until Christmas. And there's so much to do. We've got to get ready for Christmas and Jesus' coming. How are you and your families getting ready for Christmas? *As children respond, your helper will turn on the vacuum cleaner and begin vacuuming down the aisle.*

You: What in the world are you doing?

Helper: I'm getting this church ready for Christmas.

You: What do you mean?

Helper: Read Matthew 3:1-3. It tells why.

You: Okay. Let's read what the book of Matthew says. *Read the text.*

Helper: See. I'm getting this place ready for the coming king! We need to have this place clean.

You: But now? We're having a worship service. You can't vacuum during church!

Helper: But you can't have any dust or dirt when the king comes! We've got to use every minute of Advent to get ready for Christmas!

You: When the Bible says, "Prepare the way for the Lord," it's not talking about our church building. It's talking about ourselves. We need to get ready for Jesus' coming.

Helper: So I don't need to vacuum the church?

You: Not now. We've come to church to hear God's Word. And that helps us get ready for Jesus' coming. Vacuuming is a great idea, but preparing the way for the Lord happens in here *(point to your heart)* before it happens out there.

Helper: Oh, I get it. I'll just put away this vacuum cleaner and come back so I can get ready for Christmas by listening to what you have to say about Jesus.

You: Great! Now let's all get back to our seats and listen to how we can get ready for Christmas.

49. Advent Waiting

Theme: Advent; patience

Bible Text:
Wait for the Lord's help. Be strong and brave and wait for the Lord's help (Psalm 27:14).

Preparation: You'll need to decide how to integrate this message into the worship service. You'll also need a piece of Christmas candy for each child.

The Message:

*A*t the beginning of worship, explain that Advent is a time of waiting *for Christmas. There's so much to look forward to, we wish we could have it all at once. But we must wait. Explain that you're excited about the children's message today.*

Following the first hymn, stop the service and announce the children's message is so good, you want to have it now. As children rise from their seats, change your mind.

We better wait. *Then proceed with the service.*

This can happen two or three times during the service. As children rise for the message, change your mind or have another person tell you to wait. At one point, the choir director may want to shout out that the choir should sing because the choir can't wait. Tell the choir director to wait.

When the time comes for the children's message, look at your watch. Tell children the service is moving too slowly. We may need to skip the children's message. Let's wait a little and see if we can squeeze it in at the end of the service.

Just before the service ends, invite the children forward for the message. They'll be hesitant. After all, you've sent them back four or five times by now!

How did it feel to wait for this children's message? *Let children respond*. Waiting is hard! A lot of people don't like to wait. The Bible tells us that waiting for Jesus to come is one thing Christians must do. *Read the text*.

Sometimes we get impatient when we're waiting, especially if we're waiting for Christmas. We want Christmas now. But God tells us to wait and trust him.

Thank you for waiting for this message today. And because you waited so well, I have a special treat for you. *Hand out candy.*

Let's learn how to wait for God. Because when we wait, good things happen.

50. Who Was There?

Theme: Christmas; Jesus' birth

Bible Text:

She [Mary] gave birth to her first son. There were no rooms left in the inn. So she wrapped the baby with cloths and laid him in a box where animals are fed. And the shepherds saw the baby lying in a feeding box. Then they told what the angels had said about this child. Everyone was amazed when they heard what the shepherds said to them (Luke 2:7; 17-18).

Preparation: You'll need a Nativity scene with figures of the Christmas story. Before worship, hide the figures at the front of the church. Don't hide the figures so well that children can't easily find them.

The Message:

Uh-oh. This Nativity scene is empty. Who can help me find all the people and animals we need for the Nativity scene? *Have children look for the figures.*

Good! Thanks for finding everything for me. Hold on to these animals and people until I ask you for them, okay? Now how many of you have a Nativity scene at your house? *Let children respond.* What is a Nativity scene supposed to remind us of? *Let children respond.*

That's right. Jesus was born in a barn with the animals. Who has the animals? *Children hand you the animals. Put them in the Nativity scene.* Can you imagine having animals around you when you were born? Instead of being born in a king's palace, Jesus was born in a barn with all these animals.

Now, who has the shepherds? *Children hand you the shepherds. Put them in the Nativity scene.* Shepherds were poor people. Jesus loves the poor people and wants us to be friends with the poor.

Who has the angels? *Children hand you the angels. Put them in the Nativity scene.* Angels are God's messengers. They told the shepherds about Jesus' birth! We can be like angels—we can tell others about Jesus' birth.

Who has Mary and Joseph? *Children hand you Mary and Joseph. Put them in the Nativity scene.* God gave Jesus two special people to care for him. Mary and Joseph obeyed God and raised Jesus to follow God. Our parents are special to God and to us, too. We thank God for parents at Christmas time.

Our Nativity scene is almost full. But something's missing. What's missing? *Let children respond. The child who has the Jesus piece hands it to you. Put it in the Nativity scene. Read the text.*

Animals, shepherds, angels and the parents all welcomed baby Jesus. Our Nativity scene is now complete. And may you all think of Jesus on this Christmas day.

Note: This children's message may be spread over the four weeks of advent by highlighting a particular figure or set of figures each week.

51. A Visit From Santa

Theme: The real meaning of Christmas

Bible Text:
For to us a child is born, to us a son is given, and the government will be on his shoulders. And he will be called Wonderful Counselor, Mighty God, Everlasting Father, Prince of Peace (Isaiah 9:6, NIV).

Preparation: If you feel uncomfortable with the concept of this message, choose another one. You'll need someone to dress as Santa Claus. Santa will need a photocopy of this message and a sack of small toys or candy, one item for each child.

The Message:

What's the most exciting part of Christmas? *Let children respond.* People who love us give us presents. And we give gifts to the people we love. *You're interrupted by a cheerless "Ho, ho, ho" from the back of the church. Santa enters carrying his sack. But Santa looks sad and droopy.*

Look who's here. It's Santa Claus. But something's wrong. You don't look happy, Santa. What's wrong? *Santa sits with the children. He puts down his sack and wipes his brow.*

Santa: There's so much to do at this time of year. I have so many toys to deliver. I have a lot of homes to visit. This used to be fun. But I'm afraid things are changing.

You: What's changing, Santa?

Santa: People are forgetting why we celebrate Christmas. People just want to get, get, get. But that's not the true meaning of Christmas.

You: That's always a problem, Santa. But these boys and girls know why we celebrate Christmas. Whose birthday is it?

Children: Jesus'!

Santa: You *do* know! *Santa brightens up and smiles.* You know God sent his son into the world?

Children: Yes!

Santa: You know Jesus loved us so much he died for us?

Children: Yes!

Santa: And you know Jesus will live with us forever in heaven?

Children: Yes!

Santa: That cheers me up. I'm glad you know what Christmas is all about! The decorations and the gifts are great. But Jesus is the meaning of Christmas!

You: I'm glad these children made you happy, Santa!

Santa: Ho! Ho! Ho! Children are so smart. I have to get going now. I have lots to do before Christmas. *Santa hands out gifts as he speaks.* But I'll leave a little something with each of you. I hope it helps you remember whose birthday it is! *With a genuine belly laugh, Santa leaves church with a "Ho! Ho! Ho!"*

Read the text.

You: Have a wonderful time celebrating Jesus' birthday!

52. A Visit From the Magi

Theme: Christmas; the three wise men

Bible Text:
When the wise men saw the star, they were filled with joy. They went to the house where the child was and saw him with his mother, Mary. They bowed down and worshiped the child. They opened their gifts and gave him treasures of gold, frankincense, and myrrh (Matthew 2:10-11).

Preparation: You'll need gifts for the three wise men to carry. Ask three men to dress up as the wise men for this message. Make photocopies of this message for them. Ask the organist to play "We Three Kings of Orient Are."

The Message:

R*ead the text. After you finish, the organist begins to play "We Three Kings of Orient Are." The three men dressed as wise men march down the aisle carrying their gifts.*
You: Here are the wise men! Welcome to our church, gentlemen. Please take a seat with our children. *The wise men sit.* Can we help you? What are you looking for?
Wise man #1: We're looking for the king. We're looking for Jesus. We saw the star and came to worship him. Children, have you seen him? *Let children respond.*
Wise man #2: The Old Testament told us Jesus would be coming. We're excited to see and worship him.
You: Christmas is the time we celebrate Jesus' birth. Every Christmas we worship him and celebrate his coming.
Wise man #3: Great! Where is he? We want to see him.
You: I hate to tell you, but I can't show you Jesus.
The three wise men look discouraged.
Wise man #1: Jesus has already left? I knew we should have traveled

faster! You always pick the slowest camel! If we'd taken the interstate instead of those slow back-roads, I bet we wouldn't have missed Jesus.

You: Jesus didn't leave.

Wise man #2: Really? Where is he?

You: Jesus is here.

Wise man #3: Great! We've brought some gifts to give to the newborn king.

You: Jesus is no longer a baby. Jesus grew up and died on the cross. But then Jesus rose from the dead. Jesus lives in our hearts.

Wise man #1: So what do we do with these gifts?

You: Let's put them in front of the altar.

Wise man #2: Great idea. Now we can go back to the East and tell everyone Jesus Christ is living. We'll tell everyone Jesus is here! How about you, children? Will you help us tell others about Jesus? *Let children respond. The organist begins to play "We Three Kings of Orient Are." The wise men walk down the aisle to leave.*

Topical Index